MW01232644

Bright day; laughing
Your love finds us,
Inviting us to play...

Looking down, lighting
Our way, you
Radiant Star.

This book is dedicated to
Celebrating the spirit of

Heidi Ann Kremer
May 23, 1966 – June 23, 1998

Gifts of the Spirit

Experiencing Death and Loss from the Perspective of Potential

Proceeds from this book will go toward supplying books and readers to grassroots efforts to come from the perspective of potential in their communities.

PHOTOGRAPHY
Carol Anderson
Bill Clark
BJ Clark
Candi Clark
Tom Keefe
Sandra Maslow Smith
Donna Kremer Turbyfill

COVER AND BOOK DESIGN
Candi Clark

GRAPHICS & PRINTING
Candi Clark
Sunburst Graphics & Printing, Inc.
Grand Junction, CO 81503 USA

PUBLISHER
Path of Potential
P.O. Box 4058, Grand Junction, CO 81502 USA
www.pathofpotential.org

First Printing - 2004
Printed in the United States of America
30% Post Consumer Waste Fiber,
Acid Free, Archival Quality

ISBN 0-9760139-0-8

Gifts
of the
Spirit

Experiencing
Death and Loss
from the
Perspective of Potential

AUTHORS
Terry P. Anderson
Sandra Maslow Smith
Donna Kremer Turbyfill

 Path of
Potential

The Gifts

It is hoped that this perspective -the persepctive of potential- is a true gift to all who have experienced sorrow and loss.

The Perspective

"Gifts of the Spirit" is a collection of personal reflections evoked by the sudden and tragic death of a loved one. These reflections are written from the perspective of potential. Coming from the perspective of potential always begins with reflection and leads to dialogue... the aim being not to produce particular concrete answers, but rather a deeper understanding of the working and meaning of life and living. Holding the perspective of potential, we always remember that "where we come from" – our perspective – determines the life path we take and the way we live and work.

"Gifts of the Spirit" makes visible a perspective that even in the depths of our grief and loss, sees the hopeful, and lifts and evokes spirit.

X

Gifts of the Spirit
The Questions

"Gifts of the Spirit" is possible through the gift of spirit that reflecting on a loved one's death brought to us.

As is common among human beings, we too experienced and are experiencing heartfelt sorrow, anguish and grief from facing the unexpected and tragic death of our dear sister and daughter Heidi. Through this and because of this, we have come to know spirit – to experience it and taste it in ways that previously were not present to us. Through this and from this emerged a true gift, a gift of questions: Does life matter? Does our life or anyone's life matter? If our life does matter, does our way of living matter? Do we have a role and purpose... an intention to fulfill?

These questions evoked further reflections... personal reflections truly present and real to us... reflections that ultimately revealed the hope and potential that a spirit manifested brings.

We could not
find hope with
what we saw
with our eyes…
but in what we
could not see.
When we see
with our hearts,
we find hope…
which lifts us and
carries us.

3

Hope is a gift –
*   not of what we see*
*   with our eyes,*
but of what we are
graced to see with
our hearts.

*Reflection is a way of
seeing with our hearts.
Seeing with our hearts we
gain access to spirit –
such that the gifts of the
spirit become real.
Herein lies the hope – hope
for one... and hope for all.*

Discovering a Way

When our dear sister Heidi died one week after sustaining injuries in a bicycling accident, we found ourselves searching for meaning and answers to what all of our senses told us was a senseless death.

Yes, we have faith. We believe there is a Creator, and we believe there is life after the death of the physical body. Without such faith, we cannot conceive of how anyone could deal with a loss such as ours and not go crazy. It was not faith we were searching for; we are and were at the time of her death, able to reconcile to the Creator's plan the physical loss of our sister. No, faith was not our objective...but an understanding of the working and meaning of life – a way of living – became something for which we each longed. We wanted to understand the design and intent of the Creator for those of us closely affected by this tragic loss. We were searching for the meaning of our sister's death as it pertains to life...as it pertains to the lives of those still living and grieving her passing. Yes, Heidi's death evoked reflection on the meaning and purpose of every aspect of our lives.

Our faith, accompanied by the envelope of love that was built by the prayers and heartfelt caring of family, friends and even strangers, carried us through those immediate days after Heidi's accident and death. At the same time, questions - serious questions - began to emerge: Will her death as well as her life make a difference? Although she is gone from our physical world, will her spirit continue on with its work in relationship to life on earth? If our lives have meaning and purpose, then what is the way of living that is essential if we are to fulfill that purpose, and be able to give answer to the query of our life's meaning?

7

Beyond faith, and in addition to love, our lives require living hope. We have discovered as we have walked this path that hope comes to us only when we make an effort. We open ourselves to hope entering by a process of reflection.

Reflection took on various forms. Whether we chose to pray out loud or silently, to read a passage and meditate on its significance in our lives, to write a heartfelt letter to a family member or friend, or to contemplate the meaning of something, reflection allowed us to be receptive to the field of love that surrounded us all. As we entered the process of reflection, we began to see the open-ended potential in life's ongoing processes, and hope became a gift we received... a virtue especially welcomed by those of us grieving this tragic loss of our loved one. We began to see that through the Divine virtues of faith, love and hope, true healing and growth take place... and spirit lives!

Reflecting on our experience
of loss and suffering opens our
hearts to the highest of virtues
– faith, hope and love –
and particularly to the greatest
of these:
love.

All are Equal

Do not surrender your spirit to existence –
        Existence is not an end... but a means;
        Existence is intended to be an instrument.
        Spirit is your connection to the Creator.

The Creator's love works
        Through our hearts and spirit
                Such that we can become and be
                called spiritual.
In this way, we are all equal in the eyes of the Creator.

When we come together
        Heart to heart...
        Spirit to spirit,
        Our essence, our uniqueness, and our oneness
        are fully present.
        There are no races – we are all children of the
        same Creator.

As a people of earth, our common mother, and
As a people of the Creator, our Common Father,
        We are being called to come together on the
        path of life.
        On this path, the Source of which is the Creator,
            Our Common Father,
        We can celebrate and honor
                Our uniqueness,
                Our essence,
                Our oneness.
        On this path,
        It shall be as it was intended:
                All are equal.
                All have equal access to the Spirit...
                        To the love of the Creator.

By way of love entering,
the spirit becomes present
in the working of life and
in the pursuit of the
Creator's intention.

Sorrow and loss awaken within and cause reflection on the deeper meaning, intention and sacredness of life.

When searching for meaning,
we build,
not a definition of life, but
a way of living
that includes the reality of dying.

Becoming More

I have been reflecting on the process of losing a loved one from a potentializing, rather than therapeutic place. I have heard it said, "It is not what happens to you that matters, but how you handle it." What if we truly embraced life experiences as potentializing? The death of someone close to us is a huge event; it is not merely a trial to survive, but a potentially transformational event. Yes, there are stages, natural aspects, or characteristics of the grieving process. It is natural to feel profound grief, anger, sadness and lethargy. During the death process, emotions can feel so raw it seems impossible to see through to where good might emerge. There is, however, another part that is pushed aside and ignored by most... the part where self dissolves and we come out differently on the other side.

Who will we be when we rise from the ashes of grief? The obvious and popular thought is that by allowing our self to really feel the feelings associated with the loss, we will survive and be more able to return to a "normal" life – ironic as that may seem after such a momentous event.

But (and this is a big "but"!) what if we were able to envision our self becoming more than what we were before? It goes without saying that we have more sympathy and understanding than we once did; that is evident in the trusting people who "come out of the woodwork" to tell us of their own losses when we are going through the grieving process. Yet, if we add the elements of purpose and will to our grieving, there is also the potential that we could become exponentially more than we were before - we could break through some here-to-for limiting barriers and be that much closer to wholeness.

One thing the surviving family seems to cling to in times of death is the idea of gratefulness; we may think of what could have made the situation worse, or feel so thankful for the caregivers who either helped when we felt helpless, or gave our loved one comfort from pain. This grateful feeling is not just a coping mechanism; I am convinced that gratefulness and also the experience of community as we mourn the loss of our loved one are glimpses of what is possible.

One of the first benefits I gained from experiencing the loss of my younger sister was that I knew I had a soul. I had been questioning who I was and whether I had substance... and then suddenly I was discovering such deep and profound feelings within my own self, followed with the cherishing of my sister and the characteristics she embodied. From that cherishing came inspiration to develop those characteristics within me. How wonderful that we can choose to grow, and then grow. I have always understood bodybuilding this way. We can do something that results in an outward change in our body – a six-pack stomach or big biceps. This may seem gross or stupid to some people, but I understand it because I can see that it is extremely rewarding to be able to change something about our selves. In the case of bodybuilding, it is not only the body, but also the mind that changes; we become more caring and mindful as we care for and about the body.

Yes, development of cherished characteristics of our loved one is valuable not only for becoming, for example, "more playful" like my sister Heidi, but also for demonstrating to our selves that we have a capacity to nurture and develop our own minds – not just our brains, as in getting more knowledge or experience "under our belts," but our true minds. This opportunity exists whenever we meet a person with traits or ways that are different from ours; but the loss of a loved one drives the point home because there are added elements of somehow feeling that by developing, we help to act upon the purpose of the loved one's life... and therefore enhance their well being. It becomes an exchange - a chance to join with their spirit – of sorts. The meaningfulness of incorporating change and growth comes from knowing one has played a small role in perpetuating the life of their spirit. It feels powerful... like the planting of a seed.

What was once affection for my sister has become a witnessing of that about her which was pure light; wanting to take that light inside of me to light life the way a torch would light a cave... that is my intention.

Life gives us processes such as death, birth and seemingly impossible difficulties that can wake us up to how we are living and cause us to ask, "What are we living for?"

We commonly view death from a
perspective largely determined by our living
in these bodies.
From the perspective of spirit,
when perfection and
completeness come,
life in the body can end.

In the dimension of spirit,
years mean nothing...
time means nothing;
So we are free to feel joy
for the life our sister had,
for the love she experienced,
and for the difference she made for others –
both before her death and after.

*A spirit manifested is forever present
and available to the processes of life.*

Caring, Potentializing &
Dreaming of What Could Be

A spirit manifested is available forever and to all. A spirit manifested is eternal. Our sister Heidi's processes were caring, potentializing and dreaming of what could be. In her lifetime, she made real every "ounce" of potential she could. She was not afraid to dream... and seemed to have a tremendous faith all her dreams would manifest. Surely these processes are worthy of tapping... and available to all.

She was caring about all. If someone had a quirk, habit or pattern people found irritating, she would joyfully say, "Isn't that neat how Paul does this or Mary does that. They are like the appetizers in the banquet of life!" If it was the middle of a Minnesota winter and she missed the outdoors, she pitched her tent in her empty spare bedroom, opened the window, and enjoyed the air and the stars.

Now, there's faith! Not afraid to manifest a dream, no matter how little or small... no matter what others thought. She brought out the potential, and therefore hope, in so many folks... in so many ways. If you wanted to mother someone, she volunteered to be a child to you. If you needed someone to read to you, there she was. If you didn't have a family, she became your sister and didn't let you live a life alone and in isolation. "Everyone needs a family!" she would say.

Yes, her spirit is worthy of tapping... caring, potentializing, and dreaming of what could be... available forever to each and to all!

As human beings, we have the
capacity to experience life beyond
the world of existence –
to live in and from the worlds of
potential and spirit.

The ultimate expression of our
open-ended potential
  is the manifesting of our spirit.

A spirit manifested
– a heart that has
become an
instrument
for manifesting
the work
of the Creator –
is available
to all forever...
herein lies our essential potential.

Accessing Our Being

Losing a loved one is a process that has the potential to give us access to being through the reflection loss evokes; this process also holds the capacity to enable us to see the limitations of our powers, to appreciate family, and to search deeply for the meaning of life and the essence of each other. Access to being in this essential way becomes possible through an enabling energy field and with faith. How could one ever experience the potential and hope in the death of a beautiful young woman such as Heidi without faith in the Creator and without belief in everlasting life of the manifested spirit? Would this be possible without the aid of a compassionate energy field created by love and prayer?

Fearing
death,
we become
immobilized
to live -
to experience
life.

*A full life cycle
is not and
should not be
determined by the
possibilities of the
physical body,
but by the mission
of the spirit.*

The spirit lives
where there is
no time.

Purification and manifestation
are its cycles,
not the rotations of the earth
around the sun.

From Illusion to Real

Over the days, weeks and months following the death of my sister, I began to see more clearly the culture in which we are living - a culture that maintains the fantasy that none of us will ever die. The goal of living forever in a youthful body is predominant and frequently unspoken: We idolize youth and physical and intellectual processes above all else. The more we are able to manipulate the physical, the greater becomes the illusion that we human beings are and can be in control of life. We lose our connection with open-ended potential, with dignity, with life-of-the-whole, and with our own being. This culture has become so predominant that frequently even those of deep faith call upon scientific evidence to make their spiritual points.

Ironically, our culture can become more the cause of useless suffering than the relief. Our illusion that the human can live in his or her body forever can be so extreme that with each wrinkle, each ache, each weakness of memory, each loss of control, we suffer. Attachment to the illusionary physical perfection occludes our ability to see that which is more real. For below the illusionary is the open-ended potential and created dignity of each, all and everything. When we seek even more deeply, we find that which is most real and truly eternal – the spirit. Looking outerly, we may see a degenerated body – one that will soon breath its last breath. But if we see not with our senses, but with our hearts, then we may see greater spirit and future potential than we can imagine. Through reflection, we see that the spirit of a lost loved one continues to bring life and greater potential to the world after their death.

Both sensory seeing and inner seeing are open to us

each and every moment of each and every day. From which are we taking our direction? From which are we creating our patterns of living and working... the illusionary or the real?

Rather than shy away from
or build artificial protective boundaries
against the processes of life,
our work is to fully embrace,
deeply taste, and
wholeheartedly experience –

through its stages, phases,
agonies and ecstasies –
the whole of life.

Each of us has a body and spirit.
Our body will die some day.
Our spirit, however,
holds the potential of becoming stronger,
more pure, and more brilliant.

Our
body grows
without our prompting;
but our spirit grows only by
personally making an effort. The
greatest thing we can do to grow
our spirit is to open our selves to love,
hope and faith.

Opening Our Hearts

For many years, I have felt that if we are to have hope, we need to source our thinking in potential, which always sees the whole and sees the good for the whole and all of its parts. Unless we reflect on the heart of a matter, our minds and thoughts focus on parts, and are unable to create lasting solutions for the whole. We work harder and harder at solving problems and resolving issues, yet our fragmentation aids in our problems growing larger and larger. We seem to think we are independent and individual, yet in our heart of hearts we know we are all interconnected and interrelated.

This illusion of separateness leads to a focus on rights associated with possession or ownership (for example, "If I own that corner lot, I should have a right to build anything I want on it!"). This kind of thinking divides and parcels the whole world, and argues for who is the highest in having a say over what would or could be (e.g. placed on this corner lot). We do not notice this energy field in which we are swimming. We are so immersed in this sea of energies that organizes our thinking in proprietary rights that we do not even notice the strong current leading us to an existence less than what would be fully and truly human.

Human beings have the potential for being loving, caring, comforting and joyful; this was evident over the month when my family and I experienced an outpouring of humanness as we struggled with, suffered with, and prayed over my sister's hopeful full recovery, imminent death, and then seemingly untimely passing. The local newspaper printed a very short article reporting the facts of the bicycling accident, ending with a sentence, "Kremer was at fault." We all read

articles of this nature daily. It is only when we are tapping our humanness that we truly notice that the sentence is organized by an energy field of rights and
legality. From a more human perspective, one may
have ended with "Heidi's family and community suffer
the pain of her loss and celebrate the blessing of her
spirit." Is this not also a fact that is news worthy? But to
generate this thought requires we swim in a different
sea of energy than the one in which we are currently
flailing around and gasping for breath.

How can we, or how does an energy field, shift from or
evolve from one nature to another?

We know that occasionally we have the good fortune
of being in a more loving energy field. I certainly felt
this through my entire being during the months after
Heidi's accident and death. Within days of her accident, the prayers, love, thoughts and caring of rela-
tives, friends and complete strangers seemed to coa-
lesce around us, producing the collective capacity to
think from the whole, think from potential, think with
hope, and work together in a harmonious way. We
could all feel the energies working in this way, causing
us to become an integrated whole held together by
love.

If we reflect on our lives, we can see we are too busy.
We are moving too much! Our minds never stop!
Faced with tragedy, only through reflection are we
able to use the energies of grief and loss as fuel for
accessing the hope that comes from seeing the good
and the right for the future. We do not need to create
more activity; we need to create or generate reflection in the forms of prayer, meditation and contempla-
tion. A tragedy stops the doing and issues mind.
Facing injuries as great as were hers, one could imme-
diately see that chasing "who was at fault" is distract-

ing and energy-draining, and that only selfless love would enable healing and recovery. At the same time, one could soberingly see that death could also be a blessing by shortening her suffering and calling upon the love needed to find the good and transcend selfish feelings.

Reflection is a true means of accessing hope. It is through reflection we are given images that our eyes do not see - the potential good. And when we see the potential good, we experience living hope. Reflection opens our hearts to the gift of hope, inspiriting our lives and our work.

*Hope springs from a perspective that has openness – openheartedness – in it...
a perspective with potential good and the opportunity for serving the right.*

Through prayer,
envisioning, desire and growth, we will
be open to a will greater than our own.
We will not assume that what we want
is the best there could be. How powerful
it is to focus on desire for a hope filled
future rather than on how we don't
want something to be.

Hope comes through us, not from us.

A Loving Attitude

The inspiration of death is a subject not pondered nearly enough in our culture. There are three ideas that come to the forefront of my mind. The first is that by reacting to death as it comes as if it is some great surprise or shock, we, as a society or as a people, miss out on so much potential. The second is that losing a close friend or family member gives us a glimpse into the Divine nature of everyone around us. The final idea is that death is transformational (trans: beyond; form: the physical), or at least it has the potential to be, for the dying person and for his or her loved ones.

We are rapidly approaching a time when the elderly and dying population will grow even larger. It seems that this would be a good time to become conscious about death... to come from potential and to practice a loving attitude toward it, rather than shoving it aside, pretending it will not happen to us, then reacting to it once it has surprised us.

Even in unexpected or tragic circumstance, death holds the potential for an amazing grace-filled experience of human love and caring.

The benefit of thinking from potential about both the dying process and the experience of having a close one die is so great and multi-faceted that it is hard to fathom. After my sister Heidi died, I have had some revelations about death and life that have completely opened me up to accepting others and myself as being part of the Creator's divine being and doing. For one thing, I realize now that it is not so much the quantity of time I have knowing a person that counts, but rather the quality of experiences I share with them; the qualities Heidi embodied will continue to inspire me always. Another realization I have had is that we are not each here for our own development; Heidi lived just as much for me and for others as she did for herself... even her death was for us.

Christian belief is that Jesus died for us; just as many of his lessons were taught through example, I now realize that his death was no exception. We all live and die for each other... to help each other grow and develop in many ways. Separation and isolation are merely illusions of the ego. Going through the tragedy and grief of losing one so dear can either lead to a more open inspired state, or trigger a withdrawal into the false safety net of solitude; my individual reaction depends on my faith, my hope, and my openness to love. Every day I am surrounded – in streets, shops and businesses – by beings of light and love... yet do I appreciate and recognize them? Or do I waste energy by judging and dismissing them? They are all Divine creations. Sometimes, ironically, I do not know anything about them until I sit at their funeral and hear the eulogy!

The experience of going through both the bitterness of losing my ability to see and communicate with Heidi, and the sweetness of being so grateful to have had such an incredibly light person in my life, has truly transformed the way I think of and view death.

I am making a commitment to lovingly embody the characteristics and spirit of Heidi.

When someone nears death, we do what we can to help them with all of the love, care and compassion we can access. As they leave this world, the pain we feel in our hearts is so great... we do not know if we can bear it. The community of love, a gift of our human family, gives us the strength to see and celebrate the beauty and joy in a life at its physical completion... and opens for us the possibility of seeing both the power and truth of the spirit.

How beautifully we are built
– as human beings –
that we have the capacity to mourn the
loss of life. When we mourn,
our being self is awakened,
our oneness with humanity is awakened,
and our oneness with life is
ultimately awakened.

What comforts is seeing potential...
seeing there is meaning,
purpose and intentionality in life.

Through reflection
we see the hidden potential
– the hope –
in any situation,
for in the spirit of life lies hope.

Integration and Grace

Today I was given two thoughts about grieving. First, that it is not something to get over, but something to integrate. I was thinking about how I do not want to forget this experience or "get rid" of the sadness; rather I wish to get the most out of this experience... just as I hope my sister Heidi got the most out of the experience of being able to die surrounded by love, song and prayer. By seeing the loss, grieving and emotional "gamut" all as experiences to integrate, I can develop.

Second in my thoughts was the notion of grace. What we experienced a lot of during the past months was grace. The "just sitting" with Heidi and accepting the Creator's will for her was grace. The stroke that ended her doubt and suffering was grace. The outpouring of love from family and friends was grace. Perhaps it is true that within every tragedy there is a seed of grace from which potential can bloom.

To me, these two thoughts of integration and grace relate so very much to "Know Thyself," which was inscribed above the entrance to the oracle at Delphi in ancient Greece. To truly integrate this experience as a potentializing experience, and to recognize and live in the grace, I must be self-aware and I must be in the moment. Perhaps part of the experience itself places one, "kicking and screaming," into the moment; how can you not be present during such a crisis? Think of it: There are probably monks and priests in the world who spend years trying to reach the state of being we were plunged into because of Heidi's accident.

Of course, this is not to say that I am fine. I am being soft and tolerant with myself... because who knows what kinds of feelings will come over me in the next months or years; I want to be present and find room in my heart for the pain, not deny it. Only through... not with resistance... that is how I want to be moving.

She has left us forever…
And she is with us forever.
The sorrow and joy simultaneously experienced,
Awaken our hearts…
Clarifying
What is important in life
And what has meaning.

57

Tapping into Love

We sometimes try to use law to reduce our grief and anguish. Law - societal law - by nature, is not designed to tap the Creator's love; this is not its role. To access the love of the Creator requires opening our hearts in a conscious act of reflection such that we become vessels to receive this virtuous flow and transform it to images of potential. We then engage in work through which we bring that potential into being. By so doing, we begin to become truly human – we begin to manifest our spirit. Seeing and bringing forth the open-ended potential of each and all is a way of manifesting the Creator's love.

The heart that turns away from anger,
hate and fear
(regardless of its justification)
and turns to love, is a forgiving heart.

A forgiving heart is one that is receptive
to and welcomes the Creator's love.

A forgiving heart is a heart through
which love can flow between and
among us — as intended.

Consciously Choosing

We become increasingly aware that we can choose.

If we choose anger as our source...

> We walk away from and lose faith in the path of our Creator.

> We lose sight of the one and true Source... and faith disappears.

> And as the light of the true Source dims, so too diminishes our sight of the truth of our instrumentality.

> A false light illuminates our path; we begin to see our self as central.

> When self becomes central, we lose true faith and real hope... and we hazard the heart turning to hate.

If we choose love as our Source...

> We walk, regardless of the size of our steps, along the path of our Creator.

> Wisdom and understanding lie along our path.

> Understanding reveals to us the truth of our design.

> We see that each of us, all people, share a Common Father.

Each and all are intended to be manifestations of essence, gifts and truth.

We discover the truth of our oneness as a human family... and the truth of our membership in the community of life - life that springs from and is continuously nourished by mother earth.

Through understanding, compassion becomes possible... a compassion that grows through the revelation of the commonness of our struggle.

Compassion through understanding is the ongoing source of hope.

*Love flowing
is a manifestation
of spirit and serves
to awaken the
spirit of and
within each and all.*

*With spirit present
and active,
love continues to
enter...
continues to
flow.*

We are,
each and all,
designed with the
capability of becoming
perfect vessels for the
entry and flow of love
into the whole of
creation.

Only if love is present in our process
will it be present in the outcomes.

Seeing What Could Be

I am finding this first anniversary of my dear sister's sudden death to be more one of opening myself to healing and reflection than one of reliving the depths of grief and sorrow; for this I feel very blessed. Over the past year, I have learned a great deal and hopefully grown through the reflections and prayer evoked by Heidi's accident and death. Perhaps through my faith that "everything is in its place," I have not dwelled in the negative. Although I experience much sorrow and grief, I know in my heart that at the young age of thirty-two, she had finished her work in this world and was ready to move on to the next.

Since Heidi died, I have reflected much on the sorrows and joys, the anxiety, burdens and grief, and the love and dignity of life... and can see that all are gifts of life. Without trials, losses and pain, we would be mesmerized and captured by the material level of life – never searching for, never discovering the other levels of truth. We are designed and created to experience the levels of greater truth: The levels of potential and of spirit. Potential is more real than anything material; one needs only to "look" deeply into a child to know this. The truth of the spirit is that the deeper virtues of faith, hope and love are even more real than potential. If life were without loss, sorrow and death, would we ever realize we must "look up" from our existence to see the beauty of potential and love that the Creator has provided? When we "look up," we open ourselves - make ourselves as vessels - to receive the images of what could be and the grace of virtues.

Mother Teresa always said she was a "little pencil in the hand of God." She knew how to "look up." She understood that if she worked to awaken human dignity, the Creator would do the rest. Heidi's death was, and is, a source of grief and sorrow – and yet, it has caused me to "look up" and to see that existence is the least real of the worlds available to us. I am coming to see (and sometimes live in) the worlds of potential and grace opened to me through reflection and prayer evoked by her passing. I am coming to see that in whatever life gives us, if we work to see what could be and lift up human dignity in the process, we too can become "little pencils in the hand of God" – and when we do so with faith and love in our hearts, the grace of our Creator will come through in ways we could never ourselves imagine.

Living hope comes when love enters receptive vessels for the purpose of seeing what could be for the future life of the whole.

The Impossible Becomes Possible

The spirit enters our bodies, and we live a life on earth such that our self or "I" can work and develop. If the earth were so constructed that all life, once materialized, never died, we would have no interest or reason to wish or to work to transcend the ego — to go beyond self to join with the Creator in the ongoing creative work. We could become attached to the world and become completely oblivious to the Source. We could focus our attention on extraction and personal and social satisfaction, seeing no need to become instruments of the Creator in bringing potential into being. Yes, given humanity's current state of development, entropy, suffering and death help us to remember the more real part of our selves... our spirits.

The suffering experienced through our loved one's death has transformed and brought spirit to the life and soul of our whole family. Potential expanded. What was not possible has become possible. Through transforming our suffering, we gain access to the spirit... and we are nourished.

True reflection searches the heart
    for essence...
    in essence lies the intent of the Creator
        - the intent of the
        Source of our creation.

*Life becomes real when we become
instruments of the Creator in bringing
love into the world and
manifesting it here.*

*We become real when we are transformed
such that we can play a role in returning
love to the Divine Source.*

How radiant is heaven:

How brilliant and bright!

And you, my sister,
have become more
        And more brilliant...

So that your light and the light
of heaven
        Have become one light.

Life's Meaning Revealed through Reflecting on Death

I have been reflecting recently on the thoughts that Heidi's mother and I shared and discussed shortly after Heidi died from injuries sustained in a bicycling accident. These were thoughts about dying and death, including our own, precipitated by Heidi's recent death. It seems at times we were more reflecting together than actually discussing a subject, in that the aim of reflection is not to produce a particular concrete answer, but rather a deeper understanding of the working and meaning of something... thereby being more human in our thought and expression, and more able to cooperate with the intent and unfolding plan of the Creator. It is interesting that what often seems to initiate and energize the reflective thought process is a desire for a clear, black and white answer to a significant or tragic occurrence out there in the world or in our lives.

Yet, once analysis gives way to reflection, the desire and need for concreteness is replaced by the vivification and exploring of life and life processes. What emerges is something more real than the factual or so-called concrete... much like the beauty we witness in the rocks of a canyon transcends that which would be possible through a physical, scientific description of them. In a way, perhaps it is the difference between having an answer, and being or living an answer. What an amazing critter this thing called human is, when it lives - or strives to live - from the higher and more human aspects of its design, and thereby more fully lives out the intention of the Designer.

This morning as light was creeping into the valley, I felt it would be helpful to record or re-express some of that which came out of our process and processing. I will try to capture the essential notion or image we generated in regard to the death and dying of our loved ones and our selves - such that this image can be both expanded upon and deepened at a later time.

We could view life or the life cycle in terms of the visible portion (i. e. our time on earth) and the invisible portion. Our questions seemed to focus on the following subject matter: What is the transition like between the visible and invisible? What is occurring? What is the role of the living, relative to the dying – to those who are in transition? Given that we have a role and purpose on earth, do we (our spirit and soul) have a role in the ongoing invisible aspect of life?

Our reflection and dialogue was not kept at the abstract as we intentionally brought in our experiences of death and dying, particularly the unexpected or unexplainable death of a loved one. Through this processing, we arrived at some points of clarity and understanding which will provide a base for further exploration and reflection.

Being human brings with it the requirement or opportunity to experience the primary emotions of life itself; they are natural and unavoidable. Even Christ chose not to escape these emotions; witness his despair over the death of his dear friend, Lazarus. The challenge for us is to not become so attached to the emotions that we are unable to fulfill our own role, or unable to cooperate with the processes that are trying to or need to take place. An example of this for us came up when we described our experiences of preventing or holding someone back, someone in the final stage of life... who is trying to move on.

The universe is a magical, mysterious, yet knowable place; its working is complex and wisely and intentionally guided. Its unfolding creation is ongoing and hazardous, and the outcome uncertain; we have both a choice and a role in this ongoing process. Given its complexity, it is reasonable to expect that during the invisible part of the life cycle, we, or rather our spirits, have a role - thus the need for us to cooperate with the transition from the physical to the spiritual.

A spirit manifested is available forever and to all. It is not the death that we seek to connect with, but rather the spirit of those who have died. It is the spirit that we can experience, be affected by, and perhaps affect.

Death is a significant phenomenon and worthy of preparation. Prayer, meditation and reflection are processes in which we engage to prepare ourselves for death. Perhaps another reason for the slowdown experience of aging is this need for quiet reflective processes.

We cannot know what is the work of others, or when that work or purpose is fulfilled such that it is their time to depart. Embracing life and fully experiencing each other comes to mind as a guiding principle in the context of this thought.

Our thinking did bring to the forefront the realization that significant life events bring with them unique energies that would not otherwise be available to us; thus processing and gaining value from these energies becomes our work. It would seem from our dialogue that reflecting on the experiences of our selves and others, as well as exploring the thoughtful perspectives of others, was very helpful to us and aided in the right processing of these energies. It is interesting that the driving force seems to be the need for certainty or concrete explanation. Upon reflection, however, what seems to emerge is increased clarity about life and its working. We can see life more clearly, and are more able to truly appreciate it, yet it retains the nature of a sacred mystery.

With right processing, the good emerges. We can taste and experience life to much greater depths than before; we become able to appreciate and honor all of life, life's struggles, and the life force itself. We are not trying to overcome our sense of loss at the death of a loved one; mourning has its purpose. We begin to conclude that with right processing, we live from a deeper, higher, more human plane of life. If we choose to operate in the world of Will – where Thy Will always overrides my will – we can truly view the death of a loved one, our own preparation for death, and ultimately our dying, as means of becoming more fully human... such that even through dying and death, we are able to fulfill our part and participate in the unfolding plan of our Creator. Perhaps that is what realization - or becoming real - means.

Through deep reflection, what is revealed
is the truth of our earthly work and role –
work that, when carried out,
results in a spirit manifested,
thus ensuring the presence of the will of the
Creator in the evolutionary processes of
earth, life and the universe.

*We cannot know what is the
life work of others or when
that purpose is fulfilled
and it is their time
to depart.*

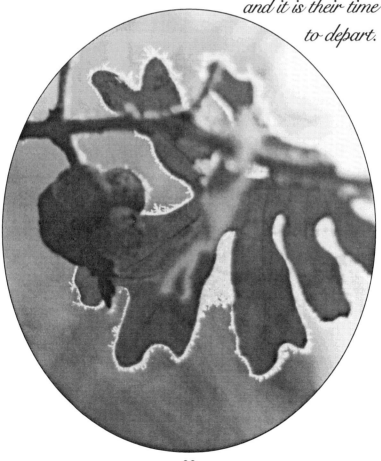

Even through
dying and death,
it is possible that
we take a part in
fulfilling the
unfolding plan
of the Creator.

The Ongoing Gift of the Spirit

When we reflect on someone's life, we can see that their death does not end their work or the working of their spirit to achieve an aim. For some, it seems that their death provides the purification of their spirit such that their work - that willed by the Creator - could be done. Death evokes reflection, and therefore holds within its powers the possibility for inspiration. Although the death of a loved one gives us untold grief and sorrow, it also opens our hearts to reflection. Through reflection, we can see that at the spiritual level, our loved one's death produces an energy field, a community of love, where we in the family might live – that is join together in faith, hope and love – and become more able to carry out the work which is our vocation and our calling.

Serving our calling,
we manifest spirit –
spirit that will be available to
all of life on earth
forever.

There is an intention within creation,
a particular way the creation is designed
and intended to unfold...
and we are, each and all,
designed and intended to fill a role in –
to cooperate with and enable -
its unfolding.

*Manifesting spirit is
at the core of the work
through which we become
that for which we were
designed and are intended.*

Life-Giving Joy of Spirit

These reflections were written in celebration of
        Heidi, a gift of the spirit.
Not in memory... from images of the past.
Not from the heartfelt sorrow and anguish we
        experienced.
They were written from the hope and the
        potential that a spirit manifested brings.

It is spirit that allows us to move beyond the
        world of material – beyond existence – to the
        world of essence.
It is spirit that awakens in us a search for deeper
        meaning – beyond the desire for answers,
        corrective action or retribution.
It is spirit entering into a receptive heart that
        makes possible the seeing of essential
        purpose, our calling, and our reason for being.
It is spirit that brings joy to life by lighting the
        path of each, all and everything.

Spirit brings life to our life, for spirit is the life force - the
        Source of all life.
Spirit is the way to see the truth of our existence; it is
        the source of meaning and purpose for our
        lives and for the whole of life.
Spirit is wisdom in action - the means for fulfilling the
        will of our Creator.
Spirit brings questioning that builds hope and
        dissipates despair.

Wherever spirit is manifested, so too is life present.
A spirit manifested awakens and evokes spirit within
        all it enters

When spirit leaves, life is gone; spirit returns
when it finds a receptive heart through which to
enter.
A receptive heart through which spirit flows into the
world and into life is available forever to all as
an eternal instrument.

A receptive heart, a willing instrument, sorrow and
anguish transformed:
A gift of the spirit.

There is good in all.
Reflective processing
is a way of realizing the good
in the sorrow and grief of death.
The good often exceeds
our understanding and
challenges our acceptance.

Books by Path of Potential
- Gifts of the Spirit - *Experiencing Death & Loss from the Perpective of Potential*

Readers by Path of Potential
- Building Your Life Philosophy - *Food for Thought* (#16)
- Dignity through Essence (#9)
- Earth Speaking (#12)
- Love at Work (#8)
- Our Choice (#14)
- Shedding Burdens (#15)
- Taking Youth Work to Heart (#13)
- The Practice of Potential - *Working from Images* (#17)
- Wholeness - Working Aim of Life (#11)
- Work for all Children - *Parenting Reflections from the Perspective of Potential* (#10)
- Working with Meaning (#7)

Path of Potential

Path of Potential is a 501(c)(3) Nonprofit Corporation dedicated to making visible the perspective of potential through publishing books and readers, maintaining a free website, and leading reflective dialogues on creating essential living philosophies.

The work of Path of Potential is supported by contributions and supplemented by proceeds from book and reader sales and subscriptions.

For additional information about the work of Path of Potential or it's publications, visit our website at www.pathofpotential.org, write to Path of Potential, P.O. Box 4058, Grand Junction, CO 81502 USA, or email: editor@pathofpotential.org.